It was on
a Monday Morning

JOHN JACKSON

LAKELAND
MARSHALL MORGAN & SCOTT
116 Baker Street
LONDON W1M 2BB

Copyright © John Jackson 1974
First published March 1974
Fourth printing March 1976
ISBN 0 551 00499 1

*For Florence My Wife
With My Love and Gratitude*

Printed in Great Britain by
Hunt Barnard, Printing Ltd.,
Aylesbury, Bucks.

Contents

Foreword

ONE OF THE PROBLEMS that constantly face a broadcasting producer is to find people who have that mysterious gift called "talent" or "star quality". This quality is very hard to define. It has something to do with helping the individual listener to feel that the broadcast is intended simply for them. Although broadcasts are listened to by tens of thousands, even millions of people, I believe that this general rule always applies.

Clergymen have a particular problem here, for normally they stand in pulpits preaching to anything from as few as ten to as many as several hundred people.

I met John Jackson in 1946. His early life until he was 27 was spent working on the railway. In those years he learned how to talk quite naturally and easily to all kinds of people and because he was a Christian he was able to talk of his faith in the same natural and relaxed way that he could talk about the mysteries of the railway signals and telegraphy to puzzled passengers and fellow workers.

After that meeting I didn't see him again for many years, then an extraordinary thing happened! I managed to get a ticket for the Cup Final at Wembley. At the end of the game as I stood up to begin to fight my way out of the crowd I saw John about a hundred yards away. I called to him — he recognised me and we fought our way through the crowd to meet. We were only together for a few minutes because he had to dash off as I did — but in those moments it flashed through my mind that this very human, straightforward, convinced Christian might have that precious gift of being able to communicate the Christian faith in terms that all kinds of people could understand.

That flash of inspiration has been proved true over and over again. For almost three years John Jackson has broadcast on "Prayer for the Day" every Monday morning. This book is the answer to countless people who have written to the B.B.C. asking for copies of the many talks he has given.

Roy Trevivian

B.B.C., London. 1973

Preface

BEHIND THIS BOOK is much indebtedness and even more gratitude. I was born into a 'rich' family, for my parents were both good Methodists. I grew up at 'top-o'-th'-hill' Wesleyan Chapel in Winsford, Cheshire. There, there were giants in the land — folk big in faith. In that chapel I met my wife and there we were married and our children were christened. No man has had, and still has, more help from his wife and family than myself.

It was a great surprise to me that I was thought worthy to be a Methodist minister and it is an even greater surprise that I should write a book. Everything worth while in my life has come to me through Methodism. So I acknowledge an unpaid, unpayable debt, for all this is the 'whence' of these broadcast talks.

Thank you, too, to the hundreds of listeners who have written to me and given me the encouragement to go into print.

My secretaries, Mrs. Margaret Legg and Miss Rosalie Poole, have persevered with my writing and my procrastinations and the scripts have come out on time!

My debt to Roy Trevivian, who taught me all I know about broadcasting, and for his friendship and the Foreword, I find to be beyond words. To his secretaries, Pat and Tina, I also owe a great deal for a great deal.

Whitechapel Methodist Mission, 1973

TANNER'S SPOUT

IN THE EARLY YEARS OF MY LIFE what seemed to me to loom largest on Mondays was the fact that it was washing day.

It began early, lighting a boiler fire, then out came a mangle like a miniature tank. There was water, water everywhere, so that dinner tasted of soap-powder. In the evening the ironing began, the irons being heated by the fire, subjected to the 'spit-test', rubbed over a piece of soap and away you dashed. Nothing was allowed to interfere with washing day. All the year round it had to be done on Monday.

I'm glad that it is all so much easier now, the flick of a switch or two, or take it down the road in a plastic bag. Any evening, any day, who cares?

But before those days that I recalled a moment ago it was even harder. My mother once showed me a valley across the fields and in that valley there was a spring of running water. It babbled on, spring, summer, autumn, winter; fresh, clear soft water. It was known locally as 'Tanner's spout', and it was over half a mile from where she grew up as a girl. On washing days, always Mondays then too in her old home, they had to fetch the water from Tanner's spout and carry it home, for they had no mains water, and consequently no taps, in that cottage where she lived as a girl.

Well, I'm even more pleased that it is all so much easier than that now, yet I wonder if we are truly grateful for the many common things which make our lives easier every day, and which all too often we take for granted? They are there to hand all the time, and we never even give them a thought, unless for some unexpected reason they fail us.

I'm going to say a prayer now to express my gratitude for many things which I shall take, and take for granted, not only today, but every day and perhaps you will want to make it your prayer too.

Prayer for the day

Lord God, please forgive me that so often I forget to say 'Thank you', for the regular blessings of this common life, which I take and use with little thought every day. Help me to become more grateful to you and all those who work with you to give these good things to me and mine.

Accept now my thanks that when I awoke this morning I could switch on a light, get up and turn a tap and there was clean, fresh water. I turned another tap and there was heat to boil the water. On my own doorstep there was milk to use, a paper to read and a letter from some of my family who are many miles away.

I am grateful, too, that from my own home I can telephone to enquire the time of a train, or if need be I could have called for the help of a doctor, the ambulance, fire or police services.

During all this time I am thankful too for the radio, for news of my fellow-men around the world, for information about the weather and road conditions, for music to enjoy, and the opportunity to join in prayer with thousands of others in this land who pause for a moment to offer thanks to you and our fellows who provide so many good things for us all, all the time.

Accept our grateful thanks now.

AMEN

WEIGHING A DOG

I'VE ALWAYS BEEN A DOG LOVER, kept them and bred them. It used to be Airedales, now I've a Boxer.

I heard about a chap once who was a dog lover and he paid a lot of money for a pedigree dog and was most anxious to do all the right things in the rearing and training of it. He soon discovered that feeding and diet mattered a great deal, and also that the diet was related to the weight of the dog; a dog weighing so many pounds needs to have so many ounces of meat per day and all that.

His problem was to weigh the dog. He tried first on the bathroom scales. He put the dog's front paws on the scales but when he lifted the back ones on, off came the front ones; he tried it the other way round with the same result. He then put all four paws on at once, but discovered that the pressure he had to exert to keep the dog on the scales gave him a false reading. He had a spring balance, but nothing big and strong enough to hold the dog. He gave up in despair.

Now there's an easy way to weigh a dog, unless he's a great hulking brute of a mastiff crossed with a Great Dane; then all you can do is to stroll down to the railway goods-yard and use the weighbridge. For the average household dog all you need to do is something very simple. You stand on your bathroom scales and make a note of your exact weight. You then pick your dog up in your arms and stand on again — again making a note of the scale reading. You take the first reading away from the second and the answer to that little sum is the weight of your dog — Q.E.D., which, if I remember my schoolboy Latin, means 'quite easily done'.

Well really I've only told you all that business about weighing a dog because I have a serious and growing concern in these days. An increasing number of folk, sometimes in the pulpits of our churches, are trying to make the teaching of Jesus and the following of Him into something very complicated, involved and erudite, so bewildering that many folk are lost or put off for ever.

For me, one of the grandest things written about Jesus in the New Testament is those words that tell us that 'the common people heard Him gladly'. Surely that means that ordinary folk listened to Him, understood Him and found joy in accepting Him as their Lord and Master and in following Him. After all, wasn't it to a little child that He gave the central place in His Kingdom? And He did say that if we want a place in that Kingdom we too are to become as little children.

Prayer for the day

Lord Jesus, help us to remind ourselves that when you spoke long ago to ordinary men and women like us they were able to understand you so well that they gave up all they had and followed you.

A smelly fisherman saw you to be God's Son; a tax-collector understood enough to change his whole way of life; a prostitute perceived in you both the truth and the way; and a soldier at the foot of your Cross got the message. Grant unto us a child-like trust and faith in you, and also obedience to you and your teaching, that throughout this new week we shall speak simply for you with both our lips and our lives.

We ask it for your Name's sake,

AMEN

MEN AT WORK

ONE WAY OR ANOTHER we all have a grouse about work. We make fun of it too, speaking of those who are work-shy as fret-workers, for they really do fret if they have any work to do. We may go on to remark that their sweat is worth a guinea — or should I now say 105 new pence — an ounce.

One such lazy fellow is reported as passing a church and when he saw a notice that read 'Sale of Work' broke out in a cold shake and gasped, ' 'Blimey, they're selling it now!'

An old boy I used to work with on the railway said that his idea of a good job was one where you started work at twelve noon and finished at 2 p.m. and had a two hour lunch-time. Most of us think that the other fellow's job is a piece of cake and far better than our own, and we could do it better than him or her anyway.

As so many of you go out to work in the morning, maybe with an inward grouse or grumble, and with what we call 'that Monday morning feeling', I want you to spare a thought for that increasing number of men and women in our land who want to go to work as we do but have no job to go to. Think of them for a minute . . .

Here's a fellow who helped to build one of the great Queen liners, but the shipyard is closed now.

Here's a chap who's just lit the fire and he looks at the coal catching light and recalls the day when the coal he burned he had got from the pit with his own hands, but the pit is closed now.

Here's a chap who was once one of a gang of twelve in a workshop. What they did is now all done by automation and only one man is needed to shove some buttons in and out.

Lots of skilled craftsmen can only sit this morning and look at their hands, hands which once made good and lasting things, but folk don't want that sort of thing now and everything is being made faster and slicker by machinery.

There's a crowd of folk here who worked for a company whose products were known and revered the world over, but something went wrong; this other crowd have no work because their workplace has been destroyed by riot and disorder, or fire.

Add to these a great company of men and women who through ill-health or injury, responsibilities to the very old or the very young, or for many other different reasons can no longer use their skills or brains in gainful employment.

So, if we've got a job and can go to it, got a skill or trade and can use it, a brain and can stretch it, let's be glad and mindful of the very many who are not so fortunate.

Prayer for the day

We who have work to do and ability to do it; something to offer and a profitable market for it; thank you God for this, and for the health and strength and circumstances which permit us to earn our daily bread.

Prosper all who deal fairly, both man and management, at their place of work.

Forgive us that in our land today there are those who would work but cannot, and guide those who plan for better days ahead, those who know the dignity of honest labour and can think beyond self and profit. Sustain those and their families who are unemployed, keep them from folly and bitterness, and hinder all whose purposes are divisive and selfish.

Lord God, whose own Son was a carpenter, breathe a new and loftier spirit into industry, that in co-operation all men may serve you as well as their fellows.

We ask it for your Name's sake,

AMEN

14

THE WORD WAS GOD

A NEW DAY HAS BEGUN. What are you going to do in it? Oh, I don't mean that you'll teach a class, mend a motor car, type some letters, drive a railway engine, or clean a room and wash some dishes. I mean something far more important than that. Let me try to show you what's in my mind.

I was in court at the Old Bailey recently. When the Judge was summing up, he said to one of the defendants that he was pleased that someone had bothered to come to court that day just to speak a good word on his behalf when he was in trouble.

There is a mention in the Bible about 'words that have put men on their feet'. Many of you may know exactly what those words mean. You were down, dejected, buffetted, even beaten, and then somebody came along and said something to you and what they said gave you new hope, fresh courage, and the will to climb back again. I could take you to a spot on the pavement of a Midlands city where just that happened to me, and it made all the difference for other words had done just the opposite.

All I'm trying to say is that, for many of us today, there may come opportunities to speak a word that can either give to someone new strength and hope and courage, or else it may well shatter their faith and shake their very foundations. If you must speak the truth, let it be in love and never be the mouthpiece for 'they', whoever 'they' may be.

If you have a criticism to make, let it be constructive. If someone speaks ill to you of another, insist that they go along with you and repeat it to the one concerned. Unless you are sure that what you say will help, leave it unsaid until you can really help. Remember, too, that the other fellow will take your rebuke as kindly-intentioned if, on those occasions when a word of praise was due, you gave it.

God Himself knew the immense power of words, for He sent His only Son here upon the stage of history to be a living word.

Men have shaped history, changed lives, broken hearts and homes, inspired great and noble deeds, all by the tremendous power of words.

So today in your world there may come a chance to speak a word to someone that will help and heal and lift and inspire — put someone back on their feet. Don't let it pass. And all those words that hurt and damn — leave them unsaid.

Prayer for the day

Good Lord, if there comes a chance for me today to speak a word to another that will help, may I not let it pass by.

If I am tempted to speak for myself or others a word that will harm, show me the sorrow I may cause so that I may leave it unsaid.

Above all, speak through me so that my words may really be your words and that with my lips, and even more with my life, I may be your messenger and in speaking put men on their feet.

AMEN

WORDS—IDLE WORDS

VERY RECENTLY severe and sudden tragedy came to the home of a good friend of ours. Oh! I know that the like has happened many times to scores and scores of people but in this case I sat down to try and write a letter of sympathy to our friend. I discovered again something I already knew so well, that is, how very cheap words are. When I put pen to paper and tried to write something of what was in my heart to him, it all read so trite and paltry and meaningless to send to someone whose heart was breaking.

The longer I live the more I'm discovering this to be true —it is indeed one of the biggest problems facing the Christian and the Christian Church today. We are all so good with words — there are endless talks, discussion groups, training committees, and mountains of words being erected as it were. Oh! I know that often they are pious words, Biblical words, theological words, erudite words, but they are still only words.

I've heard a lot of words about Ireland for a long time now as I am sure that you have. Groups have discussed it at length, preachers have mentioned it, indeed I have myself; but I know a Christian girl who is not given to polished words but she has gone to live in Belfast to work and witness there for Jesus Christ.

I've heard, too, a lot of words about Rhodesia and again groups and discussions have deliberated at great length. I know another Christian girl, not specially renowned for her speaking ability, but she is going to work and to witness for Jesus in Rhodesia.

There was a wonderful Christian lady in my last church. She went out to work long and hard, despite not being too well in health, and brought up three girls alone, teaching them to be true Christians. Also she had two sons across the Atlantic at universities studying medicine and law and she helped them all she could. She came from the West Indies. She was not especially articulate and she will live and die without speaking in public, but she could and did tell me about her Saviour with her lips but even more — far, far more — with her life. I'm proud to have known such a great lady, and yet I was very humbled as I watched her and saw her faith hold fast under great stress and strain.

What are you saying with your life? You can't hear what some folk say because of what they are. It is so easy to say the words, but it is quite another thing to go beyond that and to live it out.

God was not satisfied just to speak words, but He — THE WORD — became man, was born as we are born and grew up into manhood speaking the truth with His life. God spoke His final word in the life of Jesus Christ, and that word and that life was LOVE.

Prayer for the day

Help us not only to speak of your love, but so to live that in our lives men may see that same love in all that we do. Through Jesus Christ our Lord.

AMEN

LOVE ALL

IT HAPPENS EVERY YEAR. When it's all over, they tell us how many ices and strawberry teas have been eaten, how many folk have been there, how many hours of sunshine and hours of rain there were, and we know who are the new Wimbledon champions.

Somebody has become, or maybe has become again, world famous. Days and days of waiting, either there at Wimbledon or watching the television screen; head left, head right; groans of dismay, roars of applause, the odd tantrum or two maybe, chalk flying, judges and umpires scowled at or growled at and those annoying figures — fifteen, thirty, forty, deuce, game — oh! and I nearly forgot, *love*.

Have you ever stopped to think about the method of scoring at tennis? It's most odd, isn't it?

The first single point you gain, say one, and *only* one, ace served, and right away you have fifteen. Then you can double it to thirty. But for the next single point you don't get fifteen this time, only ten. Now you add it to thirty and it makes forty (why isn't it forty-five?). Then it's not even fifty or fifty-five, not anything numerical at all, it's *game;* unless of course you both have forty, and then you drop numbers and *deuce* is called. After that it's *advantage in,* or *out*. Oh! again I nearly forgot, there's this business of *love*.

Pure and simple, *love* equals *nothing,* and on any tennis court love always equals nothing — or, if you like, love means that you have lost. All I want to say is this, that while love means you've lost on the courts of Wimbledon, in the courts of heaven love means you've won; indeed, there you can only win by love.

In the world today, there is an increasing tendency to denigrate love, to count it as a failure, something to be laughed at, something weak; and the game goes only to the strong and powerful, those who pile up the scores no matter how; and love is to be despised and shunned.

The Bible says there are three things which last for ever, faith, hope and love. Many folk today laugh such sentiments out of court; the things that last, they say, are wealth, fame, position, power, possessions — not love. Many folk have no time for a service of love, they are quite ready to take an advantage, they don't want to be hampered by umpires and judges. Rather, they want to win at any price, and for them love means losing, as it does at tennis. You win with a fifteen per cent rise in wages; with thirty hours less work; with a forty per cent increase in dividends. Let those who will talk on foolishly about love.

I'm making my plea for love, the love as lived and taught by Jesus, and because of which He died. I'm doing it with the inner confidence that when love meant for Him a cross, and it looked as though He had lost, in fact He had won — game, set and match for all time, and all who try to follow Him now are on the winning side.

Prayer for the day

Loving Lord, help us day by day to live in your love and to demonstrate it in victorious living. We ask it for your name's sake.

AMEN

HOME BIRDS

I SPENT A DAY not far from Southend and had lunch with some kindly people in a lovely bungalow. As we sat eating our meal I looked out on to their delightful garden and saw the autumn tints on the trees — quite a change from where I now live. But I also saw something else, something that intrigued me and took me back many years to my boyhood and youth in Cheshire.

You see, the man in the house next door to where I was lunching kept pigeons, and he had a rather splendid cote for them too. Much smarter than many that I recall when I was a lad.

Fascinating birds are pigeons. When I used to work on the railway I saw baskets full of them taken off the train. The porter then took the basket to the end of the platform, pulled the wooden peg out of the wicker-basket door, and released two or three dozen birds. After circling around the station a time or two, off they flew, straight as an arrow for their home.

I used to go and have a look sometimes at the labels on the baskets and saw that they had come from sixty, seventy, eighty or more miles away. I know for a fact that at that time there used to be a very big day in the life of the pigeon fanciers — a race from the south of France back home to England. To win that was a real feather in one's cap — if that is a proper thing to say about pigeon fliers.

These amazing birds always go straight home — or nearly always. I recall a platelayer I knew who was having a lot of trouble with his birds. They were not coming back home, but getting lost somewhere, and one of his mates suggested that he should cross them with a parrot and then when they got lost they could ask their way home! I daren't tell you his reply — but anyway, as a rule, pigeons do go home.

I can't help wondering whether these words may reach somebody who has also left home — just walked out, cut yourself off from your family and loved ones. You might have done it in temper or in haste, in sulkiness or in shame. You blame them, and they blame you. You spoke about managing on your own. 'All right, I'll show them.' you said; or you could be thinking. 'They will never have me back after what I did and said.'

Or else it was from your home that someone cleared out. Perhaps you told them to go, perhaps you begged them to stay, but they went, and it's hard to forgive and maybe even harder to forget.

A rather wonderful thing happened the first Christmas that ever was. Because of a census being taken, and the way in which it was organised in those days, everyone went to his own home town.

If your family has been split up, how wonderful it would be for you and yours if you did just that — if you went home and were reunited. No blaming, no judging, no inquest, no recriminations — just starting off afresh together again, the family complete and whole under one roof.

If what I have been saying has been especially on your wavelength, if you are separated from someone — well, it is always time to go home, and God bless you and yours.

Prayer for the day

Lord Jesus, you came to an ordinary home, to humble people, that first Christmas that ever was, and you brought love.
May all of us find love and unity in our hearts and homes.

AMEN

BY COMPARISON

PROBABLY MOST OF YOU follow a daily routine of getting up out of bed in the morning, shortly afterwards leaving your home, and later on in the afternoon returning home again. You've got a home to go from, and to come back to.

I've made some new friends recently and none of what I have just said about you is true about them. They have not got a bed, or a house and home, and not even digs or lodgings. They sleep rough, if at all, they all dread the colder and wetter nights.

Most Sundays, my wife and I and a few others in turn have our tea with them. They come to us, some eighty to a hundred of them, and they are very grateful for a wash, a sit down and a very plain and simple tea. But most of them didn't get out of bed, more likely out of a doorway. They didn't leave their home, they just wandered this way, and at what is bedtime for us they hope to find somewhere fairly dry and not too cold.

Why am I bothering you with all this? Well let me tell you a true story. That great preacher, Charles Haddon Spurgeon, was once visiting one of his church members and for over an hour he listened to her as she moaned and grumbled about her troubles and trials — and all of them added up didn't amount to much. Spurgeon never said a word as she grizzled on. At last he stood up, got to the door, and turning to her said, 'Good afternoon, and forget not all His benefits.'

I want you to begin ignoring the debit side as it were, all those things you haven't got, and to concentrate on the credit side. As an old hymn puts it, 'Count your many blessings, name them one by one.' Add up all the good and grand things you've got and remember that compared with my Sunday tea-time friends you are very wealthy indeed.

Oh! by the way, one of the things I've noticed about my new friends is that they are always ready to share fag ends with each other and to divide even next to nothing by two. I look forward to my Sunday tea nowadays because I'm quite sure of this, that every Sunday now I shall meet Jesus in church.

Prayer for the day

Forgive us, Lord, that often we take great benefits with little thanks and many good things every day as if they were our rightful due. Make us more grateful and more mindful of all those who have little or nothing.

For Jesus Christ's sake.

AMEN

SAY 'THANK YOU'

I'M SURE THAT LIKE ME you can name a number of people who have given you a great deal of happiness, pleasure and amusement in your life. For all of us, surely, there are those who do this in many spheres. For my part the list of such folk grows and grows each year.

Gilbert Harding was one whom I liked very much — no frills or fol-de-rols; no sham and veneer — open, frank, honest, and for those who knew of his illness, there was good reason for his going maybe a bit too far on occasions. You remember he died quite suddenly and it has always been a deep sorrow to me that I never bothered just to drop him a line, if only a post-card, to say 'Thank you', when in some programme or other I had been especially pleased as I had listened.

No one's writings have ever given me more pleasure than the novels of Howard Spring — I've not only read his books but re-read them over and over again, and from them received a great deal of pleasure. But in his case too he died and, alas, again I had never bothered to write and tell him of the pleasure he had given me. When it was too late I was very sad about it, but there was nothing I could do.

The other writer I would want to put alongside Howard Spring is Sir Neville Cardus, that prince of writers on cricket (most of which I can understand and fully appreciate) and that eminence of writers on music, which I am beginning to understand only little by little, and still go on trying. I've turned the pages of his books and lived over again some of my boyhood and days of my youth in the sun at Old Trafford. What a debt I owe him! But in his case I did write and say 'Thank you', and got a lovely letter back in his own handwriting. I treasure this.

Well, you remember I was saying that probably all of us have people who down the years have given us much joy and pleasure. Do you ever bother to thank them, to express your gratitude in no matter how simple a way? Sometimes I think we live in a grumbling and grousing age. So many folk seem to like to moan; so many folk seem all too ready to put pen to paper and write a complaint, to express disgust, to point out someone else's deficiences, to expose another's faults. All too few of us are ready and willing to praise, to thank folk.

Indirectly I think that here we may be very near the heart and secret of happiness. There will always be plenty to complain about but my plea is that we look for the things to be glad about and grateful for, and that we never defer or neglect an opportunity to tell someone of our gratitude for the pleasure or service they have given us. One can, as I have said, leave it until it's too late.

Prayer for the day
We thank Thee, Lord, for all those folk who in scores of ways make life brighter and happier for us. Let us ever be grateful to them and let us never put off telling them so. For Jesus's sake.

AMEN

FOR EVER BOUND — FOR EVER FREE

WE HEAR AN AWFUL LOT THESE DAYS about liberation and freedom and allowing folk to do their own thing — no interference, no discipline — free expression and so on. As with many things I have a suspicion that there is a grave danger here. Grave because so much of what is being asked for, or should I say demanded, is good; in fact so much is often so good that it obscures the evil that is also present.

I recall an evening long ago when I worked on the railway. I was just ready to go out one evening when I was called back to work. Actually, the trouble was very near the station in my home town and I got along there as quickly as I could. I shall never forget the sight that greeted me: it was a railway engine (a proper one I mean, in the days of steam), but where do you think it was? It was lying on its side in a field by the railway line and a lot of goods vans were either with it or on their way down the embankment. One or more of these vans was filled with eggs, or had been before the crash, and, my word, there was stuff enough for an omelet for all the world and his wife lying about.

Briefly, what had happened was this. At this station four lines, one up fast and one up slow, one down fast and one down slow, ceased to be four lines and reverted via some points into two tracks only. The engine driver coming along the down slow line had read the down fast signal as his and kept on coming. The points were not set for him though and he ran up the sand drag into the buffers, and even that didn't stop him. On he went and over on to its side went the engine into the field.

I often look at my little grandson, aged three and a bit, and think what a pity it is I shall never be able to take him to see a steam engine roaring along at seventy to eighty miles an hour, for all the romance of railway engines has gone, for me at any rate. I've watched the *Royal Scot* and the

Coronation Scot steaming past that place where the engine lay in the field and it was magic to see such power hurtling, along the lines.

Ah, yes! But while the engine was free to do that all was well, but when it was free from even the lines, and could go just where it pleased, it hadn't gone many yards before there was disaster. Often entire freedom can be a very dangerous and harmful thing.

And do these folk who shout about freedom really want us all to be free? Do they want to meet me, because I feel like it, hurtling towards them on the wrong carriageway of the M1 doing seventy miles an hour?

Do they want me on the football or cricket field to be free to play according to my own rules and not the book?

Do they want the fellow next door to rape their sister, or give their young brother drugs, just because that's the thing he's doing at the minute?

Do they want everyone where they live or work or play to be free to do just as they please: the boss not to pay wages one week; the bus not to run home; the canteen to open only when someone feels like it; the bonuses and overtime to be at someone's whim and fancy; the profits and dividends to depend on chance?

I'm a nonconformist and proud of it, I'm a free-churchman and proud of it, but I still want to see engines running only on railway lines, I don't want them in fields or in Euston Road or Lime Street.

Jesus was a great believer in freedom. His kingdom is a kingdom of freedom, but freedom within His rules of love — love of God and love of one's neighbour as oneself. Yes, I too believe in freedom — like that.

Prayer for the day

Lord Jesus help us so to love you and follow you that we may find in your service perfect freedom. For your Name's sake.   AMEN

PRAYER

DID YOU EVER HEAR THE STORY of the little boy who was out for a walk with his Dad and Mum and, as little boys often do, he kept running on ahead and sometimes he hid behind a bush or lamp-post and sometimes he just waited. Once, when he ran ahead, he came to something quite new to him, a telephone kiosk. There was a man inside using the telephone and he had left the door open. The little chap was amazed and simply stood there staring and listening until his parents overtook him again. Then he said, 'Look, Dad, there's a man in that glass box talking to himself.' Well it could quite easily have seemed like that to a little boy.

There are, however, a lot of people — adult people, not little boys, who feel that when folk say their prayers that's exactly what they are doing, 'talking to themselves'.

There are others, and I'm one of them, who know that isn't true. Down the years, you see, we've put it to the test and proved that the God in whom we believe is a God who both hears and answers prayer. There have been countless thousands too, in every day and age, who believed this and they have proved it in their own experience.

But even we who so believe have found there is always something to learn about prayer, and I want to share with you something that has been a great help to me, and still is, in my own prayer life. It's this: there are many different ways in which God answers prayer. Here are just four of them.

The simplest way, and the one we like and covet most, is for us to pray and for God to answer, 'Yes'. This does happen and it's a grand experience.

But you know, it is equal evidence of His hearing and answering when He says 'No'. For if you stop to think about it there are many times in our relationship with other people when the only answer love can give is 'No'.

Another answer I have found God gives to me from time to time is for His reply to be 'Not yet'. I'm rather an impatient fellow often and this isn't how I like things, but the One who decided an acorn should become an oak tree is a very patient God indeed.

The last answer I want to point out is the answer, 'If you will, I will'. God can only play His part as and when we are willing and ready to play ours. Isn't this very clear in the prayer we so often use, 'Forgive us our trespasses as we forgive those who trespass against us'?

No, we're not talking to ourselves when we pray. God always does answer in His way, though not always in ours.

Prayer for the day

As your first disciples asked, so do we: 'Lord, teach us how to pray.'

AMEN

AMAZING GRACE

I'M SURE ALL OF YOU will have had, at some time, the horrible experience of being the first one who is too late. You left it a bit late to nip out for the fish and chips for supper and the person in the queue in front of you had the last of the last fry. Or it might have been strawberries, or a ticket for a show or a football match, or a shirt or a skirt in the sales. Well, it's bound to happen with most things and the reason is very simple; there's a limit to the supply. Only so many chips are fried, or strawberries grown; available seats stop at a certain number and goods for sale cannot exceed stocks in hand.

But the other day I got a bit of a shock. I was passing by a shop and in the window was quite a large notice and it read *'Amazing Grace* — no stocks available until next month.' Well, I suppose it was true in a sense because the shop was a record shop and they must have sold all their records of *Amazing Grace.*

But the 'Amazing Grace' of the song, you know, is the Amazing Grace of God and this is one thing on which there is no limit. In fact, I know a hymn that says:

> Grace is flowing like a river,
>> Millions there have been supplied.
> Still it flows as fresh as ever
>> From the Saviour's wounded side.

Let me remind you about this grace. Somebody once described it as 'the love of the loveliest falling on the unloveable and making it lovely'. I think that's great, because it means it comes from God to me, to make me like Him, and what's true for me is also true for you.

Let me remind you too of something else about grace. There are folk who live in what are called 'grace and favour' residences; they have no right or claim to do so, but the privilege is granted to them.

Or again, you or I may make a claim from our insurance company, but when all the facts of our claim have been examined, it turns out that legally we have no claim at all. But sometimes the insurance company says it will still make a payment under the circumstances. So, while we have not the slightest entitlement to it, they give us some money and they call it an *ex gratia* payment; it's given without being earned or merited, freely from grace.

Do you see now why it is right to speak about 'Amazing Grace'? It is truly amazing that God deals with us like this, not legally, not based on merit, deserts, understanding, logic or reason, but 'graciously'. He always has done this, and He always will; the supply is endless and for all who will take it. God gives grace.

Prayer for the day

The grace of our Lord Jesus Christ be with us all, evermore.

AMEN

FETCH DAD

A LITTLE WHILE AGO I went to preach in Huddersfield. I hadn't been there for over twenty years and I want to tell you of something that happened on my first visit there.

I was then minister of a church in the East Riding of Yorkshire and we, that is the men of the church and myself, were busy with 'do it yourself' jobs in the church, painting all the exterior and the inside; amongst other things we were making a more modern entrance. We had been offered, by a church that was closing in Huddersfield, a large mahogany screen with plate glass in it — just what we needed. One of our chaps who had a lorry, and a number more of us, went over to dismantle, collect and bring back the screen.

Well, we got it free, the screen I mean, and all in one piece. Eventually, with a deal of trouble and bother, we had it out on to the pavement and the lorry was drawn up alongside. Now the next thing was to lift it up and place it carefully packed on the lorry and away back home.

Well, we tried and tried, huffed and puffed, but there just were not enough of us; not sufficient strength to lift that weight, that high, on to that lorry.

Now, all the time we had been struggling and heaving, a few children had been standing watching as might happen anywhere. Amongst them there was a little lad and just at the point when it was plain, even to a little boy, that we couldn't do what we were trying to do, he looked at me and said, 'Wait a minute and I'll fetch me Dad.' Then he ran off across the road and into one of the terraced houses there.

Shortly afterwards he came out again and his Dad with him, a great big fellow about six foot two and weighing fifteen stone, with hands like dinner plates. We all, plus Dad that is, had another go and in no time the screen was loaded safely and then tied down and off we went. But we were only able to do it with outside help; us, plus the father.

I've found that true so very often. There have been many things I couldn't manage, in my private life, my work, my relationships, until I went to my Father, to God and asked for His help. I have been hopeless, useless and defeated, but once I called Him in, and all that means, once I took Him at His word, according to His promises, then and only then did I win through. Remember that today and always — all things are possible with God's help, and He's willing and waiting to help and guide us all the time.

Prayer for the day

Help us always to come to you for help and ask you to fulfil for us your gracious promises. Forgive us that all too often we try to go it all alone. We live as though your faithful promises had never been made to us.

AMEN

TWELFTH MAN

I AM A LOVER AND A FOLLOWER OF CRICKET, and it goes a long way back. Far enough back to recall as a schoolboy lying on the grass at Old Trafford and once touching Maurice Leyland's flannel trousers as he was fielding on the boundary. Come to think of it, I believe I refused to wash my hands after that for several days. 'Days in the sun', Sir Neville Cardus calls them, and that was true in every sense, even at Old Trafford!

Well, as the test matches come round and I read the team and compare it with my own selection, I think about that obviously necessary selection referred to in cricket parlance as 'the twelfth man'. It's a queer sort of job, nothing at all like the substitute in football who at least might be on for part of the game. No, the twelfth man is a real dogsbody. He might be a runner, or do a bit of fielding in a none too specialist position, or you may see him carry on to the pitch a bat, a pullover, a cap or a tray of drinks. They might even change him, substitute a sort of thirteenth man to let the twelfth man go home, in fact you might go right through the game and never even see him at all. What a job!

Rather like an actor who's never on the stage but always messing about in the wings — no name, no fame, no glory.

Yet he must be there and he must play his part, humble and obscure though it be. By not doing so, by being missing when he was wanted, he could let the side down, and let it down sadly.

Now I know lots of people who feel that their lot in life is just like that. Sometimes it's in the home, sometimes it's at work or in the church; they think they don't matter. If you feel like that I want to say a word of encouragement to you. It's this: all service ranks equal in the sight of God. What you do, if it be right and good, matters, and if you don't do it, or if you do it badly, you let the side down.

I don't think Wellington won Waterloo, I think the ordinary soldier did. I don't think the Kingdom of God comes because of the big names. I think it comes a bit nearer every day because in the lives of so many ordinary folk there is something Christlike, an image of Jesus. When will Christian Britain come? Never, if you don't play your part.

Prayer for the day

If our lot seems humble and small and of no import in our own eyes, or the eyes of others, remind us that in your eyes, Lord Jesus, it really matters in the extension of your Kingdom, and that we all have a vital part to play.

AMEN

CENTRAL HEATING

IN THIS COUNTRY we're never short of something to talk about, for when all else fails we can mention the weather. Our climate is always good for comment if it isn't good for anything else. Someone I know blames all the bad weather on 'them space men'. I don't know to whom she attributes the good days.

I suppose the main concern of all of us during the winter is keeping warm. A dear gentleman I've heard of in the West Country in the days of the last war, heard you could, under certain conditions, get extra coal. He applied and received a great big long form to fill in on which he had to give, or was supposed to give, a lot of details as to why he wanted extra coal. All he wrote were four words: 'To keep me warm'. He signed it, sent it, and he got his coal, I'm glad to say.

Many of you will know that Methodist ministers like me are provided with a house and some furniture as part of their stipend. None that I know expect a mansion, but nevertheless some of us have, and have had, heating problems.

You can imagine my joy when I tell you that this winter, for the first time in my life, we've got central heating. Oh! boy, what bliss on a cold and frosty morning! But you know, central heating isn't a modern innovation. It was available in the eighteenth century, and what is even more amazing it was also available in the time of Jesus.

Let me tell you about it. In the eighteenth century John Wesley went to a meeting in Aldersgate Street, not very far from where I live. It was the month of May and yet when he related what happened to him at that meeting he said amongst other things, 'I felt my heart strangely warmed'.

Someone writing about him in a book, remembering this, called him the 'Knight of the Burning Heart'. It all happened because that day in the City of London John Wesley came to know Jesus Christ as his personal Saviour and he knew that his sins were forgiven.

Now to go back to the first century. One day two people were walking home from Jerusalem to Emmaus, a village seven miles distant, and somebody walked and talked with them on that journey. He went into their house for a bit of supper and then, only then, they recognised the stranger as Jesus. Even though it was bedtime they went back — seven miles mind you, and on foot — to Jerusalem to tell their friends the wonderful news that Jesus, who had been put to death on a cross, was alive again. He'd been with them and then, they said, 'Did not our hearts burn within us as He walked and talked with us on the road?'

Again the reason for the heart-warming — the central heating — was Jesus.

But, you know, countless thousands of folk have found this to be true and are still doing so. It's happening every day, that once you let Jesus come to live and to rule in your heart, as your Lord and Saviour, you find your heart is strangely warmed and life is never the same again. No matter how icy cold may be the blasts of circumstances, nor how freezing and chilly may be events or people, you have this inner glow that Jesus brings with Him to everybody who will receive Him. I hope this is the kind of central heating you've got.

Prayer for the day

> Come into my heart Lord Jesus.
> Come in today, come in to stay.
> Come into my heart Lord Jesus.

AMEN

HONOURS LIST

WHEN I WAS READING the latest honours list I recalled to mind a radio programme of some years ago. In that programme Wilfred Pickles used to interview members of the audience and ask them questions — most interesting questions they were, too. Among the questions was one which, when he asked it, invariably brought fascinating answers. The question was, 'On whom would you like to pin a medal?'

If *you* had the power and the authority to award medals to people, what sort of people would you choose, and why?

This all came back to me as I was reading the honours list this year, and since then I've been quietly awarding my own medals to different people.

First, there's a girl I met in Yorkshire over twenty years ago, named Betty. If it wasn't on her honeymoon, it was very soon afterwards — her husband became paralysed from the waist down. She was smiling through in those early years — ah! yes — but I saw her again last year, over twenty years having passed, remember, and she's still smiling and still has both her faith in God and her love for her husband. Yes, she got one of my medals all right.

Then there's a lady I know who has been a Sunday school teacher for longer than I've lived, and she kept in touch with her scholars when they were grown up and away in the last war. She gave up recently as a senior teacher, but because they were short in the primary department she went in there to give a hand. There's a lot more I could tell you about her that deserves a medal, but for me she's a real lady, is Florence.

There's a Doctor of Divinity who didn't think it demeaned him when he played the piano for the primary department of a Sunday school.

A man injured in a road accident three years ago is still on crutches. But in a letter to me last month he said he's still trusting the Lord Jesus.

Finally, there's a man who was a veterinary surgeon who I'm sure could have made a great deal of money if he had so chosen, but instead he worked for the P.D.S.A. and every moment of his life was dedicated to sick animals, often those who belonged to the poorest of the poor. Often they were quite unattractive mongrels but he dealt with them all as though they were potential Cruft's prize winners. Indeed I'm sure his all-too-early death was due to his complete love and service to dumb animals without thought at all of self or reward. What he did, he did because he saw it as a part of what it meant for him, indeed a major part of what it meant for him, to be a Christian. I presented him with a medal even though, alas, it is posthumous — a great and good man.

There are many who have loved and cared for, in their own home, aged, sick and sometimes awkward, ungrateful parents or other relatives over many years and never thought of putting them in a home or shirking their responsibility.

There are all those who have, as we say, 'got on', and have been unspoiled by it and never forgotten or despised their origins.

There are all those who would rather do something for nothing than always to clamour for fame or name or gain. A medal for all of these in *my* honours list.

Prayer for the day

Lord Jesus, give us eyes to see the truly good and great people around us, and may we find in them an example for our own lives. For your Name's sake.

AMEN

WHEN SILENCE IS NOT GOLDEN

WE'VE GOT SOME ODD SAYINGS in our English language, sayings about cooks and broth, horses and drinking, red skies, sows' ears, penny wise, birds in bushes, glass houses and the like. I've been thinking recently about a very well known idiom 'Silence is golden'. I wonder if it originated with the chap whose wife said to him, 'George, we've been married twenty-five years today, how shall we celebrate?' and he replied like a flash, 'Let's have two minutes' silence!'

Well, perhaps it didn't start there, but it doesn't matter. What does matter is, is it true? I don't think it is, always. Guilty men have hidden behind silence. Cowards often take shelter in it. Frequently it is a shoddy tinsel or veneer. It's dangerous because its opponents are not able to fight back cleanly and in the open, for all men to judge if it be a fair fight or not. All too often it belongs to the realm of neutrality, it has a tepid mediocrity about it and those who keep it are to be seen sitting on the fence. They won't stand up and be counted, never saying 'Yes' or 'No' but playing safe: no after effects for themselves or their cronies.

One of the things I'm sure about is that this is not where the followers of Jesus belong. Jesus Himself never practised such expediency, in fact if He had there would have been no crucifixion. For Jesus silence was not golden whenever or wherever there was evil.

In these days of blurred edges on so many standards, when grey has crept in more and more, and we hear less and less about black and white, to be lukewarm is the vogue rather than being hot and cold.

I'm increasingly sure that the Christians in the world have got to say so. It's not good enough just singing 'Stand up, stand up for Jesus', or 'I'm not ashamed to own my Lord', there's a desperate need for us to speak out. If we encounter wrong in national, civic, industrial or family life, yes and in church life too, let us say so. Jesus spoke out, in the lanes, at the fishing nets and in the temple. Men were not left wondering, or guessing, or bewildered about where He stood: they knew clearly and plainly. Today many people try to solve, and are concerned about, the problem of communication. It's a major problem in the Church and all too often we say nobody's listening when it would be nearer the truth to say nobody's speaking.

The Gospel is bold and incisive, it has a tang, a cutting edge, in the presence of evil. Do away with that aspect of it and we shall wither and die even faster than we are doing now.

Prayer for the day

O fearless Christ, so plain your voice,
    It spoke both plain and clear.
Make us prepared to make a choice,
    Rid us of cowardly fear.
When you did see the sins of old
    You said that they were wrong.
May we today be strong and bold
    To speak out brave and strong.
Give us your strength to follow then,
    Not weighing up the cost,
As true and frank and honest men.
    Though all things else be lost.

AMEN

WHAT'S IN A NAME ?

I'VE BEEN THINKING quite a bit of late about names, and the longer I have done so the more fascinating it has become. The subject is colourful and conjures up amazing pictures and possibilities. When I was a boy I had a few holidays in a lovely village near to Bedford, it was reputed to be the second prettiest village in England. I spent hours watching the skill of the blacksmith, the roaring fire and the flying sparks, and he had the perfect name for a blacksmith; he was Mr Goodhand.

Years ago I was driving through a town in the north west and saw a sign — Dolittle and Dally. I'm sure it wasn't literally true, but what names to belong together! I remember a railway signalman christened Albert Edward Ferguson Montgomery, and a lad christened Vimy Ridge because his father lost his leg in battle there in the 1914-18 war! I've heard of Sidebottoms who, as they say, 'get on in life' and become *Siddebottarms*, and I remember a man in Crewe railways works whose name spelled Onions to me but he insisted it was *O'Nyons* — well, so be it. When the late Jesse Boot became a peer he took the name of the river of his home town and became Baron Trent. My Dad said at the time it was a blessing he hadn't been born in Stafford for then he would have been Baron Sow — fancy that!

Some folk say there's nothing in a name; call a thing what you like, it makes no difference. I'm told my heart is a pump and pumps blood around my body — so is yours. I don't think I should get away with it, nor would you, if we held our nearest and dearest very close in the moonlight and said, 'I love you with all my pump, darling.'

For me names are not only interesting, they are also important. I belong to a group of folk who have been about now for two thousand years. They are all alive some here

43

on earth but the majority in heaven, and we rejoice in the name of Christ and are called Christians. It's a name high over all other names. Today's version says we are 'the Jesus people'.

It's not only our job to tell people but also to show people; it's not just a matter of labels, it's a matter of life, of living. You can plant a dog rose and label it Super Star or Dorothy Perkins but as it lives and grows the lie will out. So we can bear the name and live and grow not only to be unworthy of it but even to bring it into disrepute.

I wonder sometimes if we ought not to drop the name Christian and speak only of being Christlike. Would that help us perhaps to realise more fully that we have a Name to live up to?

Prayer for the day

We who call ourselves by your name, Lord Jesus, ask you to help us to be always worthy of that name.

AMEN

GOLDSMITH

BECAUSE I HAVE A DEAR FRIEND with the lovely name of Goldsmith I have been reading up something about goldsmiths. It takes us back to 1607, for in that year the Court of the Goldsmiths' Company issued an ordinance about apprentices, young men learning to be skilled craftsmen in the art and mystery of the goldsmith.

When the young man has completed his apprenticeship he is expected to produce for the warden of the Company a 'masterpiece' to show that he is not — I quote now — *'of the idler sort who betake themselves to the sole practise and exercise of one slight and easy part of the said mystery, but is able to finish and perfect a piece of plate singularly with all garnishings and parts thereof without the help of many and several hands.'*

Isn't that old language beautiful? And what a challenge to all of us! Surely the followers of Jesus want their lives to be a masterpiece, a piece fit for the Master. Well, this relic of the Guilds of Old England reminds us that it takes time — you serve an apprenticeship not just of seven years but a whole lifetime.

Also, following Jesus is not a matter of 'the sole practise and exercise of one slight and easy part of the said mystery'. I find it very easy from time to time to be Christlike in one instance that is slight and easy. I've given a copper to a blind man and a drink to a man at the door, and an old coat or two to refugees and indeed the odd pound here and there for a good cause. But to go on and on, and to finish and perfect, oh! that's another matter. To make my life like His all the time, all the way, and, what does it say, with all the 'garnishings', so that it is winsome and attractive — my word, that's a lifetime's work, isn't it?

But there's the last bit, 'without the help of many and several hands'. So you see the apprentice goldsmith is on his own. He must not expect, solicit or receive any help on pain of disqualification.

Well, wonderful craftsman though he be, this is where we part company with him.

Yes: we have an apprenticeship to serve, like him.

Yes: we need to aim at perfection.

Yes: we need to remember the garnishings.

But: we don't have to go it ALONE. Indeed, if we did, we should fail, but the wonderful thing about Jesus is that those whom He calls, He also equips; because He is able, He also enables us. We may be weak, but He is mighty. He has promised us His power, His presence, and so day by day He works in us and through us. He removes the dross from our lives, He refines us until He looks at us, and if we will we shall shine, a perfect masterpiece. Then He, Jesus, will look and love His image in our lives.

Prayer for the day

Perfect us in all good things, Lord Jesus, until Thy beauty is seen in us.

AMEN

A LAD OF MINE

I WANT TO BEGIN by telling you two stories. The first I heard myself not too long ago, and the second is a story my father told me many years ago which I've never forgotten and I hope I never shall.

The first was something which happened in a home I was visiting. When I called, mother and boy were at home and I soon gathered mother had had one of those mornings with the lad. He'd really been playing her up and she was getting to the end of her tether and she told him so, in my hearing, in no uncertain terms. She ended up by saying, 'God doesn't love naughty boys, does He, Mr. Jackson?'

She expected me to say she was right, but she wasn't. So I said, 'Yes, He does love naughty boys, and naughty grown-ups too, but He doesn't love them to be naughty' — which is a very different thing. You see, if the mother was right, then God doesn't love me and I know He does.

Now my father's story. A man had a very wayward, indeed wicked, son. Over the years he, the son, had been in all sorts of trouble, in the courts, in prison, and yet each time the father had welcomed him back home again and given him another chance to make good. This went on for a long time and then the lad got into further trouble, the news of it broke out, and as usual it was the talk of the neighbourhood. While it was the topic of everyone's conversation a man met the boy's father.

'I hear that lad of yours has been in trouble again,' he said.

'I'm afraid he has,' said the father.

'Ah,' the other fellow said, 'I know it's not the first time by any means. I know all you've tried to do for him in the past, but I gather the offence is worse than ever this time, isn't it?'

'Aye,' said the father, 'I'm afraid it is.'

'You know,' the other chap said. 'Do you know what I'd do if he was a lad of mine? I'd put him out smartly through the door, shut it, and then turn the key once and for all.'

'Aye,' said the father. 'Do you know, *if* he were a lad of yours that's exactly what I'd do, but you see I can't because he's a lad of *mine*.'

Yes, God does love naughty boys and girls and He never turns them away because they are always lads and girls and men and women of His. He calls them His own — always.

Prayer for the day
Lord Jesus, help us all to know that we belong to you, and that we can never be beyond your love and caring, nor can anyone else.

AMEN

BOB

I'VE HAD REASON to think a great deal recently about my old golfing partner, the finest anybody ever had. I'll tell you why I say that in a minute.

A few weeks ago I read that Lee Trevino said it was no use playing golf unless you also had time to see the flowers. When I saw him a few times on the television I was amazed how happy and relaxed he was, even in international tournaments, and above all how he enjoyed every minute of it. When I read about the flowers I knew why.

Well, my partner was like that. As we went round together he would always stop and we'd talk about the things of God, a word in the Bible, a line from a hymn, our sermons, our families, our future, or even a football match. I remember once standing still with him for ages while together we watched a sunset, 'lost in wonder, love and praise'. Because we played golf like this we never really knew or cared who won, but nobody was happier or got more out of a game of golf than we did. I often thank God for every minute we spent together to the enrichment of my life and experience.

A man I know who is very rich, so rich he retired early and then had an illness, told me once it wasn't until he was ill that he had ever noticed three things:

Birds singing.

Trees changing colour.

Clouds moving across the sky.

He had lived well past middle years and he had been so preoccupied with his work, with making money, that he had never noticed any of these things at all.

I said a moment ago he was very rich and by his standards my old golfing pal was very poor. Yet in my heart of hearts I know that I ought to put it the other way round. It was

4

my pal who was truly rich, for he possessed the things that really matter, the things no man can give you and no man can take away from you, things that never perish, things which belong not only to time but to eternity.

When put to the tests that life, yes, and death, bring, I know who will be able to stand the test. You see my pal loved Jesus and served Him as His faithful minister.

Prayer for the day

Lord Jesus, grant unto us a true sense of values and teach us to covet and to hold only those things which make us rich in your sight. For your name's sake.

AMEN

GOING UP

ON MY WAY HOME FROM THE NORTH, as I was driving down Watling Street, the A5 in the Rugby-Daventry area, I noticed along a good stretch of the road fields and fields of masts and aerials of all shapes and sizes. A sign on one of the gates said it was Post Office property. I've since made a few enquiries and found out that these masts towering up into the sky are used to enable messages to be sent round the world. In the north where I'd been staying I could look out of the bedroom window and see the T.V. mast at Winter Hill — high up into the sky to make it easier to transmit T.V. into folks' homes.

One of the features now of a visit to London is the Post Office tower, well above the normal London skyline, so that telephone messages can be got more easily from the metropolis to the provinces.

On holiday in Cornwall a year or so ago we went to Goonhilly and there they send their messages thousands of miles up to a satellite in space and then back down again to earth.

Most of us are left breathless when we listen to and watch men on the moon, almost as though they were on the lawn next door.

Well there it is. It seems that in order to do more things and to do them better, and indeed to do some of them at all, it helps if you go up; the higher the better.

Do you know that, in spite of what a lot of people are saying and writing these days, I still have no problems in thinking about God as 'up there'? For me God is no myth, nor is He dead. In fact as far as I know He's not even been poorly.

Further I've also found in my life that the more I go up to Him, as it were, the more effective I seem to be down here.

When I blunder on alone at an earthly level I don't seem to get very far at all. I'm soon exhausted of ideas and lost and bewildered and quite ready to chuck it all in: to give up and say 'Well what's the use anyhow, who cares?' Yet when I get up higher, when I speak to God and He speaks to me (and He does), it makes all the difference.

Danny Allcock in my home town used to sell lump salt and he went round the streets with a donkey and cart. Then one day he went round with a wheelbarrow and somebody asked him, 'Where's the donkey, Danny?'

'Why,' he said, 'I'd just got the stupid thing used to living without food and he went and died!'

A lot of folk are dying at an earthly level because they never reach to God for food, for power and purpose, for light and love. You might do a lot better this week on the horizontal if only you gave more time and thought to the vertical.

Prayer for the day

God our Father, we reach up to you in prayer and ask you to be with us down here. Feed us so that we may continue to live as you meant us to do and so grow more like you every day. For Jesus Christ's sake.

AMEN.

REMEMBER TO FORGET

I TOLD A STORY on the radio a few weeks ago about a girl who used to bring a shilling back to my grandmother and ask for another. Well, believe it or not, I've had a message from her. She's an elderly lady now, of course. Her name is Polly and she was thrilled to bits to hear on the radio about her girlhood days. She remembered her visits next door with those, or should I say that, weekly shilling.

Yes, she remembered. I've been thinking a lot about memory — maybe it's because I suspect my own is not quite as good as it was. I used to flatter myself that I had an excellent memory but maybe *anno domini* is taking its toll. Now I need to recall the saying that the palest ink lasts longer than the strongest memory.

What sort of things do you remember? What have you got stored away? What do you recall to mind most often, most readily? What are those things you are most anxious to store and cherish, for ever if you possibly can? I'm sure that our answers to these questions would reveal the kind of people we really are, they would be true guides to our inmost character.

I want to make a plea for you to remember something, something very important. I want you to remember to forget. Now I have found this very difficult, especially in recent years, and yet I know full well that I ought to do it.

Remember to forget injuries past. It's so easy to brood on them, to keep bringing them out and turning them over until they grow even more sour and bitter. We need to remember to forget these for our own sakes.

Remember to forget the worst in people, their meanness, pride, pomposity. We sometimes so dwell on these faults in other folk that we grow quite blind to the fact that often in those same people there are traits that are good and wholesome and praiseworthy.

Remember to forget to moan and groan. How easy it is to keep in mind all the ills of life, all the dark days, all the problems. These all come to most of us with the passing of time. Yet to store them up, and indeed add them up in our memory, spoils our outlook; our vision is impaired and we see life with a jaundiced view, a view far from the truth and out of all perspective.

Well, memory is a wonderful gift. You can use it, someone has said, so that you can have roses in December or, if you like, mistletoe in May. Or you can use it not to remember roses at all, but only thorns. So let us remember that there are some things we need to remember to forget.

Prayer for the day

Lord Jesus, help us to remember only whatsoever things are lovely and honest, pure and true and of good report. For your Name's sake.

AMEN

SPEED IS NOT EVERYTHING

ONE OF THE MANY JOYS that come to a Methodist minister is due to the fact that it is an itinerant ministry and we move around from place to place. Because of this some of my years in the ministry have found me ministering in the country and numbering farmers and farm workers among my people. Indeed some of my finest friends belong to this community. Only they will be able to tell if I have, over the years, ministered to them, but I know that over those same years they have ministered to me — and I don't mean the sack of potatoes, the piece of cheese, or the pat of butter.

The good farmer has always made me ashamed of my impatience. I like to see results, to see things happen and to see them happen quickly. If I put in extra effort then I tend to expect extra speedy returns. In a way I suppose I want to till and plant and harvest in the same week, if not in the same day.

My farmer friends are not like that. Quietly they go about their work and equally quietly and patiently they let the weeks and even months go by before they even think of harvest. Sometimes I've know them make a second sowing of this or that and have to wait still longer for results and returns.

Living in a day and age in which increasingly speed has been almost deified, when it is assumed that all too often that the faster also means the better, we do well to question this. To recall that speed is not everything everywhere. Perhaps we who live in our cities, and especially we who live in the metropolis, need to know that the farmer often waits and waits a long time for his due reward.

Have you ever thought about the patience of God? The Bible puts this great truth in a very colourful way. It says

God is 'long-suffering to us-ward', and my goodness, what a blessing that is! It means He goes on puting up with me, He's patient with me, He's prepared to wait for me to improve, and though He's been waiting a long time already He will go on waiting.

Maybe there's someone you know, someone in your home or place of work, with whom you tend to grow impatient. Oh! you may well have been tried and pressed for a long time. Well, keep it up, don't let your patience run out. It could be they can only keep going because of your quiet tolerance. There will come a day when the result proves it was all worth while, so for now just go on patiently.

Prayer for the day

Thank you, God, for your patience with us. Help us also to be patient with one another.

AMEN

SHERBORNE

I HAD A GREAT PRIVILÈGE SOMETIME AGO when I was invited
to preach at the Sunday evening service at one of our
greatest public girls' schools. For me it was a sort of red-
letter day in my ministry. I had never been in that part of
the country before and it so happened that I went down
there the weekend after the late Archbishop of Canterbury,
Dr Fisher, had died. He was remembered in the school with
great affection and I enquired what he did in these latter
years of his life after resigning from the highest post of his
particular branch of the Church. I was told, and the person
who told me was well qualified to know, 'he was just a kind
of curate and happy to be such'.

Many people have paid just tributes to Dr Fisher, but for
me none will ever surpass that simple tribute: an archbishop
happy to be a curate. That's about as near as you could get
to the spirit and teaching of Jesus this side of heaven. I shall
always be glad I was invited to Sherborne, for several
excellent reasons, but I'm glad I came to hear from the local
folk there of this great and good man who was truly humble.

I find that this spirit of humility is all too rare today, and
what is even worse, it is all too rare inside the Church, indeed
within the ranks of the ministry. Time and time again I find
folk who are obsessed with their status, concerned about
their rights; ruled by pride and self-centred, very often to
their own and other people's hurt, too.

I have read and re-read the New Testament, and especially
the stories of Jesus, and I find that the only right I have as
His follower, is the right to wash other people's feet. This
was the pattern, the example, which He left for us. This
lowly status and only this lowly status is ours by right.

With all his learning and scholarship, with his exaltation
to the highest office in the established Church, with his long

and intimate royal contacts and relationships; with all these, and everything else beside, Dr Fisher in the eventide of his life was content to fill a place of lowly service in the name of Jesus. He would know that in the end that was what really mattered. All he had done before that was only of worth because he could and did lay it all aside and end as he had begun, in the lowliest rank of all in his Church, there to serve and to minister to those in need day by day.

I think perhaps the world would both understand and respond to the Church today if only it could see us free from all concern about status. Rid of all pomp and ceremony and paraphernalia, of dress and ritual, we should instead be doing what Jesus did — laying aside our garments and taking a basin and towel.

Prayer for the day

Thou dost require of us that we do justly, we love mercy and we walk humbly with thee. Help us so to do, O God.

AMEN

CLEAN UNDERNEATH

A CHANGE OF CLOTHES, clean and fresh to begin the new week, is the normal pattern for most of us, I guess, on a Monday morning.

My mother was always very keen about our being, as she put it, 'clean underneath'. To underline its importance she would often add, 'Suppose you got knocked down in the street and were taken to hospital.' For her the shame of being found dirty underneath was too terrible to contemplate. It was not enough to be spruced up to the nines and looking right and decent on top. What could not be seen was far more important in the end than any top or outside show.

Now, she was not only right, but I think she was more right than she knew. I know now that she really spoke in a parable. Far more important than in relation to our clothing, I think it matters a great deal what we are like underneath.

Hundreds of years ago God sent one of His men on a mission. He had to go and visit a farmer who had several sons and to annoint one of them as King.

The man saw one or two smart, upright, kingly-looking chaps and thought one of them must be God's choice. But God spoke to him a great truth and said, 'Man looks on the outward appearance, but God looks on the heart.'

That is still true. We've all known folks who looked right outwardly and then we've discovered, sometimes to our cost, that underneath they were far from right. They wear a covering of tinsel and veneer, a sham or fake goodness, yet just below the surface there is a mean spirit or a hateful pride, an intense greed or selfishness. Quite often they say 'Lord, Lord', but they are not really the Lord's people and sooner or later the true self underneath comes out, and it's dirty.

The old pirate ships used to sail under false colours. They *looked* like friends and then suddenly their true colours were seen, but too late to be countered, and the pirates achieved their wicked ends.

There is a desperate need in our world, our land, our town and sometimes even our church, for those who are of solid worth, the same through and through, clean underneath, utterly reliable and sincere. You can smarten up your appearance with clean clothes on top, but not your life, your character. And in any case, remember, God looks on the heart.

Prayer for the day

Make us in your image, Lord Jesus. May we be sound and good through and through. May we be what we profess to be and always free from sham and subterfuge and pretence. Help us always to remember that while we may often deceive our fellows, nothing is ever hidden from you. Through Jesus Christ our Lord.

AMEN

A NIGHT OUT

WHEN YOU GET TO MY AGE you don't jump up with a great thrill of expectancy at the suggestion of 'a night out'. In fact my work has been such over many years now that I've increasingly grown more and more thrilled when the possibility of a night *in* loomed on the horizon!

Even so, sometimes a night out does come along, as it did for me quite unexpectedly recently, and it was a real treat, I assure you. We went to a show and then we finished it off with a meal. My goodness, we counted it a real treat, something to remember with gratitude for a long time to come.

For the average man, if there is such a person, I suppose you can get some idea of what sort of person he is by asking him how he spends his evenings. What does he do when he comes home from work, has a meal and then — *what?* The answer will tell you a great deal about the kind of person he is.

I keep bumping into folk, usually my own age or older, who make sweeping statements about young people today and often seem to write them all off — wholesale. I can't accept this. Have you noticed that we're living in a time when more and more folk are giving up their spare time to working for and helping other people? Thousands of people give thousands of hours every week, not for themselves at all but utterly and completely on behalf of somebody else.

In one week recently I stayed in two different houses. The chap in the first one is often out in the evening, sometimes travels quite a few miles, to repair and adjust tape recorders and record players for people who are blind so that they can enjoy the Blind Book Library facilities. I thought that was splendid, but was sorry to hear they are short of qualified people in some parts of the country willing to do this. Oh! there's no pay.

In the other house the chap there had had a night out, and also a call during the night, because he supports the Samaritans and mans the telephone and also takes emergency calls. Both of these men go on doing this, month in, month out, year in, year out — spring, summer, autumn, winter.

It gives me a thrill to know such folk, folk for whom a night out is something for somebody else, not for themselves. You see, to me it seems they are getting very near to the spirit and teaching of Jesus who kept on reminding men that they must forget themselves and remember others.

Well now, just give it a bit of thought and see if you can't arrange with Jesus to have a regular night out for somebody else.

Prayer for the day

God bless the folk who help and serve other people rather than themselves, and make me one of them.

AMEN

A WELL AT WESTMINSTER

OVER THE YEARS I have been on a number of occasions, and for various reasons, to our Methodist Metropolitan Cathedral, the Westminster Central Hall. Yet until a couple of weeks ago I didn't know a remarkable thing about that building. I knew it was in there that the first meeting of the United Nations was held, but this was something far more local and domestic.

I was there for an evening meal and was going to speak after the meal. I sat next to the minister and he passed me a glass of white wine, their own brewing he said. Then he told me that under the City of London there are a number of natural springs, artesian wells, and one of them is right under the Central Hall, Westminster. It provides them with their own private water supply and this is what he referred to as their own-brewed white wine. It was rather fascinating to think that the cool, clear water which I was drinking was a special and private supply just for the church there.

Some years ago I went to the Holy Land. It was in August and for me the heat was almost more than I could stand. I was amazed, too, at the arid dryness of the land and the burning sand of the wilderness was quite frightening. Yet it wasn't until I saw this for myself that I even began to realise why there is so much emphasis in the Bible on the value of water. Indeed, not only was water priority number one for life, but when the Bible talks of a vision of heaven there is still this great emphasis on water; flowing streams, a never-ending supply, never, never being thirsty.

I suppose then it's quite natural the Church should speak about Jesus as offering the water of life, of satisfying men's thirst once and for all, of a supply that never dries up.

Well in the end it's all picture language but it enshrines a great truth. In Jesus is offered a satisfying and an abundant

63

way of life — every other way is only a substitute and often a poor substitute. His way, as offered by the Church, is a sort of spring from inside, like the well under Westminster Central Hall, which if men will accept it, is sufficient.

I wonder if what you're working for, running after, dying or striving to get, buying sometimes at great cost — I wonder whether, if and when you've got it, it will really give you what you hope for? Having attained it, will all longing cease so you really begin living? Two lines of a hymn fittingly describe the plight of all too many folk today — 'The waters of the earth have failed, and I am thirsty still.'

Why not give Jesus and His way, His teaching and His rules of love, a try in your life? Many would loose their fears, their follies and their futility if only they would do this. It's not only at Westminster for them, it's everywhere for all, including *you*.

Prayer for the day

Lord Jesus, we come to you in our need, for wherever else we have gone we have never been fully satisfied. Help us in our thirst for goodness, to drink of you, the Fountain Head, and so never thirst again. For your Name's sake.

AMEN

GOSSIP

WHAT I WANT TO TELL YOU ABOUT actually happened on a Monday many years ago now when we were living in the Potteries.

At the church where I was the minister we had a Women's Meeting on Monday afternoons and my wife attended this meeting regularly. One Monday, just before lunch time, we noticed a pool of water on the hearth in the dining room. We wiped it up and in next to no time it was there again. Then we knew the worst; we had got a burst in the back boiler. I raked all the fire out and threw the red hot ashes on the garden. I took out the fire bricks and the grate-iron and there, sure enough, was the water steadily oozing out of the tank for the hot water at the back of the grate.

We sent for the plumber and he said he'd come right away and we realised all too well we were in for a right old mess of water, soot and plaster. I had to go out in the afternoon and my wife said to me, 'Just drop into the women's meeting.' So I did just that, poked my face round the door and said to all and sundry, 'Sorry Mrs. J. won't be down to the meeting today we've got a leak.'

A couple of weeks later I met a lady who belonged to our church and who had not been for several weeks. So I stopped and spoke to her and said we'd missed her and asked when was she coming back and what had kept her away. She turned suddenly on me and with a fair old glint in her eyes she said, 'Never mind bothering about me, talk to your own wife. She can go to Leek Market on a Monday afternoon and miss our women's meeting, so you begin with her and leave me alone.'

Well, I suppose, 'got a leak' and 'gone to Leek' sound much alike when spoken to all and sundry in a basement

5

room at the chapel and it was really all only a misunderstanding. Yet it could have been really hurtful and might have done harm.

I heard a chap say recently, speaking of two boys, 'They both stood there and never said a word.' You see he didn't know they (the two boys) were both deaf and dumb.

How easy it is to make snap judgments, to pass hasty and hurtful criticisms, to misquote what we've heard, or only think we've heard. Sometimes it spreads and grows, and often it loses nothing in the telling and repeating, but usually goes from bad to worse.

This way, you know, friendships have been destroyed, homes and families have been broken, churches have been split in two and many folk have had untold and unnecessary suffering: all through gossip. Innocent people have had their characters taken away, and sometimes they have not even known what they're supposed to have done or said.

Many years ago now I read a bit of good advice. I don't know where it came from originally, but I think it's worth while passing on to you. Here it is: Before you pass on anything about someone else, ask three questions:

> Is it true?
> Is it kind?
> Is it necessary?

Prayer for the day

Forgive us, good Lord, if anything we have ever said has hurt someone else. Help us always to look for the best and may we not repeat what may be untrue or unkind or unnecessary. For your Name's sake.

AMEN

RED LETTER DAYS

I NOTICED ON THE NEW CALENDAR I have in my office that certain days are marked in red while the majority are in black print. It reminded me that we sometimes speak of certain days as red-letter days, because, like those picked out on my calendar, there is something different, something special about them.

Those that belong to our personal lives, yours and mine, are the days on which for us there was an event ever to be remembered. We got engaged or married, our first child or grandchild was born, and year in and year out as those days come round we remember that they were red-letter days. No two of us perhaps have the same reason for marking off a certain day in this fashion.

I remember in my teens seeing a play at a London theatre in which one of the characters, a lady it must have been, at a certain time, began to have a bad chest. After that she spoke of such and such having taken place two or five years 'before me chest', or three or ten years 'after me chest'. For her all history hinged around that day in her life when she began to have chest trouble. Well, as Frankie Howard would say, 'Poor old soul.'

The founder of that branch of the Christian Church to which I happen to belong had a red-letter day. It was May 24th, 1738, when in Aldersgate Street he accepted Jesus Christ as his personal Saviour.

St. Paul had such a day too when, on the road to Damascus, he gave his life unreservedly to Jesus.

Yes, and there's a multitude which is quite beyond counting of men and women, in every age and in many lands, who also lay claim to a red-letter day in their lives. For all these it was the hinge of history for them. After that nothing was ever the same again.

Yet I don't suppose that any of them, as they began that new day which subsequently became a red-letter day, had any idea at all that it was going to happen. They may have thought, 'Ah! well just another day'; and then the great thing happened. I wonder what this day has in store for us? What will happen before nightfall? I wonder if today is going to be a red-letter day?

I never cease to wonder at the fact that God must like the ordinary people because He made so many of them. The story of His Church is by and large a story of His calling ordinary folk from their fishing boats, their tax office, the loom, the market, the plough, the hospital and a thousand and one other commonplace jobs. On a red-letter day they respond and are used by Him to shape history, to change the lives of many others, to bring His Kingdom nearer.

So if your life seems humdrum and futile and meaningless, keep alive a spirit of expectancy, of readiness, lest this day, or indeed any day, is going to be your red-letter day. I'm sure that for all of us there is to be, if it has not already happened, a day or days that one day we shall look back on as memorable — a red-letter day.

Prayer for the day

Give us, Lord Jesus, the spirit of contentment, yet also of readiness; the willingness to serve you well just where we are, but also the knowledge that you may call us to greater things and so to live each day remembering it could well be *this day*.

AMEN

'BLEEP - BLEEP'

Since coming to live in London I've got something I've never had before in my life. I find it both useful and fascinating and I get quite a kick out of it in a way. I feel I've got a rôle — oh! I know it's only a minor rôle — in this marvellous electronic age in which we live. This thing that I've got is called a 'bleep'. I'll tell you more about it in case you should think it's Val Doonican's 'favourite toy'.

I'm a chaplain at the great London Hospital. Not only is it great in its works of healing, research and training, but it's also great in size. I still get lost in it and still there are parts where I've never even been yet. When I go in on my visits I go to the Hall Porter and say, '145', and he gives me my 'bleep'. It clips in the top pocket of my jacket and stays there all the time I'm in the hospital. Now if anyone wants me anywhere in the hospital, or indeed if someone should ring up for me from outside the hospital, this thing goes 'bleep-bleep-bleep' in my pocket and I get in touch with them straight away.

So you see, wherever I am I'm never out of touch, never out of reach. It is always possible for me to get in touch with the heart of things at any time. There's a sort of line of communication between us everywhere, all the time.

Yes, in a sense a bleep is something quite new to me, and yet it isn't. For many years now I've had a bleep in a way. You see, I've always known that anywhere, any time, I was in touch with my Lord and Master, Jesus Christ.

It is such a pity that for many folk prayer, being in touch with Jesus, is just something for a special day or time, or special words or special books. For some it's even worse, they have no thought or knowledge at all of any line of communication twixt earth and heaven. For some there once was a line but now it's broken, for one reason or

69

another, and the only sound they seem to hear is just the mocking echo of their own voice.

I want you to begin opening up or re-opening the lines of prayer, the communications between yourself and Jesus. I want you to prove for yourself, as I and countless men and women in every day and age have proved, that 'He walks with you and He talks with you as you travel along life's way.' I want you to know that you need never be utterly alone, that He wills and He wants to keep in constant touch with you. I want you to know that when you need Him most He is nearest at hand. I want you to know that for you Jesus can be nearer than breathing, closer than hands or feet.

Oh! By the way, I mustn't forget to tell you something else about my bleep at the Hospital. From time to time it has to be recharged, or else there comes a day when the contact and the communications will cease. You'll remember that won't you.

Prayer for the day

We thank you, Lord Jesus, that you both hear and answer prayer. Speak plainly to us and forgive us that so often we think we can 'go it alone' and fail either to get or to keep in touch with you.

AMEN

HERSELF

I WENT BACK RECENTLY to a town where we lived for seven glorious years and it brought back many wonderful memories. Amongst them I recalled a man who would ring me up and say, 'Eudokia speaking.' He was a great elderly Methodist minister whose name was Goodwill. He was a scholar too and had done outstanding service as a missionary in India. He loved his Greek New Testament and always gave his name in Greek — Eudokia. When he rang he always said why, but always before he rang off he used to ask, 'And how is *Herself*?' It was a strange way, but it was always his way, of asking about my wife.

Had he rung up a week or so ago I should have had to say, 'She's not well, she's had a bad fall, strained some ligaments and for a week or more could not even move around the house.'

Well, when that happened the lot didn't fall on Jonah it fell on me. I became promoted overnight to head cook and bottle washer. It wasn't too bad at first. There was stuff in the fridge and in the pantry and I opened tins and defrosted and fried and even managed a bit of dusting, flicking a feather or two around like, quite sharply too.

But then I soon found you don't only get the lunch ready, you have to think about tea and supper and next day and the day after. And then there's early closing in the shops and they only have steak pies Monday and Thursdays, even dog meat and dog biscuits don't go on for ever and folk call and folk ring up. Always it seemed to me that I'd two things nearly boiling over on the stove, and the potatoes aren't the same without salt in the pan, and custard can be anything from the density of water to a likeness to yellow plasticine.

I had my moments of glory. A crust on a rabbit pie and a chocolate cake she'd promised for the Sunday School

...ty, they turned out grand. Not from the cookery book ...ethod, but the 'advice bawled from the bedroom method'.

Anyhow, why do there have to be two sorts of flour, and why is it I can make non-stick pans stick, and why do things boil over so quickly one day and take so long the next, and who was unloading all the city of London's dust in my flat so that if I left it a day or so you could write on the table top 'clean me' in the dust?

After about six days of it I'll tell you my ligaments were getting strained too, and I wondered if I qualified for a home help, or who'd wheel me a meal or two round. I'd just put my feet up for a spell after a meal and washing up when the dog would look at me and want to walk, mind you. And then too there was my shopping list and 'Have you made the beds?'

'No I haven't,' I said. 'It was all right when I got out this morning.'

What I'm really saying is a special word to all you chaps, and it's this. Remember to say thank you to Herself, be it wife or mother. Don't take for granted all they do day in and day out. Two or three weeks of it would put most of us men on our backs or out of our minds. Yet all too often we come and go and take it all as a matter of course, and we don't even pause to think until one day Herself can't do it any more and the lot falls on us. Our prayer could be 'God preserve us,' but instead —

Prayer for the day

We thank Thee, Lord, for those who day in and day out look after us in our homes; for all their loving service not only make us grateful but remind us from time to time to say so. Through Jesus Christ our Lord.

AMEN

72

SIGNPOSTS

A WEEK OR SO AGO I went to the seaside on the east coast to preach, and between the afternoon and the evening rally I went along the sea-front. There's a bit more ozone there than there is on Whitechapel Road and I thought I'd give my lungs a treat.

I noticed a signpost in a very queer spot, not a cross roads or anywhere that seemed to lead somewhere or call for a decision regarding which way to take. When I got near enough to read it I was amazed. It said, '2,546 miles to the North Pole'.

I went and sat down on a bench in a shelter and pondered on it. I didn't want to go to the North Pole and I couldn't think of anyone who would, not starting from there anyway. I couldn't see any significance for me in knowing how far it was. Well, I suppose there is a reason for it being there; a purpose quite unknown to me for pointing the way and giving the distance, but I'm still quite lost about that point and purpose.

I can recall the days during the last war when for fear of enemy invasion all our signposts in this country were either removed or obliterated, and this presented some folk with quite a few problems if they needed to journey over unknown roads and to strange places.

But there are not only useless signs about, or even no signs. Sometimes there are wrong signs about. I vaguely remember reading about a man who was dying and was also obviously distressed. The reason for his deep concern was that a memory had come back to him in those final hours. He recalled that when he was very young he had gone to a signpost somewhere that must have been fairly loose in the ground. He had managed to hoist it round in its socket until

73

the arms were pointing in the wrong directions and the places on it were not the way the sign said. Indeed the signpost was now telling lies. His big concern was, had anyone gone wrong, been badly mislead, by what he'd done those many years ago, and had it caused them hurt or harm?

I wonder what happens to folk you and I are leading as parents, teachers, employers, older people in our place of work? Nearly all of us have got somebody who is taking their directions from us, especially if we are parents.

Can I ask you, will it be all right for your children, or indeed anyone else, to follow you along the road you've planned to go? Are your directions going to be good, and wise, and pure, and true?

Prayer for the day

Lord God, who hast given us the right way in Jesus Christ, may we so follow after Him that anyone who follows us may journey in joy and safety. Help us never, ever, to mislead another on the Road of Life. For Jesus Christ's sake.

AMEN

REPEATERS

WE HAVEN'T got a lot of pictures in our home — apart, of course, from photographs of the family, especially grandchildren. But there is one picture that I cherish, it's a colour plate of the old L.M.S. railway engine *Royal Scot*. I rode on its footplate once years ago, but that was in the days when there was romance in a railway engine and when you watched them roaring down the bank at Betley Road at eighty or ninety miles an hour.

But, alas, steam has gone and now it's boxes on wheels like a cubist's impression of a giant stag with antlers. Gone, too, are many of the signal boxes and also the majority of the old semaphore signals. Some of you will be able to recall what were called 'distant signals'; as the name implies they were some distance from the signal cabins and they were painted mainly yellow and had fish tails. Now, you know, it was not only the job of the signalman to pull his levers and to see that the signal was then in the OFF position, it was equally important that when he restored the lever in the frame, after the train had passed, he ensured that the signal had also returned to danger.

There was often a snag here, for either these distant signals were too far away for him to see, or sometimes they were out of sight around a bend in the track. To overcome this, a simple but very effective electrical circuit was used. It was connected to the mechanism of the signal, and in the signal cabin itself was a miniature signal. This little signal was called a 'repeater', for it repeated, for the signalman to see, the position of his out-of-sight distant signal. Incidentally it also repeated, for the hours of darkness, if the signal lamp was ON or OUT. Very important for the safety of so many were these repeaters, enabling someone to see what was happening out of sight — a true replica in fact.

There are a lot of us in the world today who are proud to call ourselves by the name of Jesus and say we are Christians. You know, I'm sure, that this means we ought to be repeaters. That anyone who wants to see Jesus, and lots of folk do, well, they ought to be able to look at us and see a replica — somebody like Him.

I wonder how much of our thinking is Christlike; how many of our words are just the words Jesus would use; how often our deeds are repetitions of the kind of things which Jesus did. I grow more and more convinced every day that this is what being a Christian means. It is possible for us, too, because He would never ask of us the impossible. The world is waiting for such *repeaters,* of this I'm sure.

Prayer for the day

Help us, Lord Jesus, to follow your example, to pattern our lives on yours and so to reveal you, our Lord and Saviour, to our fellows.

AMEN

THANKS FOR EVERYTHING

I'M SURE THAT MANY OF YOU, like me and mine, will have been fortunate enough to have had a holiday this year. Down tools, pack up and away from it all; be it north, south, east or west, here or overseas, it was a change and a break. I think I'm more grateful than ever this year to have had a holiday, for so many of the folk we meet and minister to in my Mission never have had a holiday at all. There are even lots of children about us who have never seen green fields, a cow or sheep or donkey.

To me it is very interesting to see what folk reply when I say to them, 'Back from your holiday then?' And go on to ask, 'Did you have a good time?'

Some reply, 'Grand, only one bad day, lovely food, splendid company, beautiful scenery.'

Others say, 'Rained all Tuesday and Wednesday of the second week — queer woman at the next table — noisy kids on the beach — always somebody else picnicking in the lay-by's — back again — can't tell you've ever been away — the old grind still waiting for us when we returned!'

Well I suppose the grumblers can't help it, or maybe they have got a good reason I don't know about. Sometimes I get the impression that they even get some pleasure out of moaning and groaning, but in the end I'm sorry for them. You see, they are so much the poorer and they are living life at a loss as it were.

Less and less folk, it seems to me, have a sense of gratitude. This was brought home to me on my holidays when for the first time for many, many months I went to the cinema. It was a fine film, but one of the things I shall always remember was the incident of a man under political pressure having to leave his country. He had to leave behind all his possessions, his land, property and the like, and he was only able to take what he could carry. He had a horse, a rather poor old thing nearly at the end of its days, but it had served him well through the years. He went into the stable, fed it for the last time and gave it an affectionate pat as he said, 'Thanks for everything'. Real gratitude; and gratitude only does become real when it's expressed, when it is shown.

There are so many things for which you and I should be grateful. I hope we are, and even more, I hope we say so.

Which reminds me of a little girl of two who has just begun to say her prayers, and her prayer will do to end with today.

Prayer for the day
Thank you Jesus.

AMEN

BLIND TRUTH

VERY NEAR to where we stayed on holiday on the south coast there was a very big and lovely property standing on the hillside and looking, as it were, out to sea. Perhaps that sounds a bit silly because you know, and I know, that buildings don't look out to anywhere. True enough, to be sure, but people in them do. Well, I suppose that as a rule they do. Yet it makes it even more silly in this particular case because it wasn't even true of the people, for this lovely place, situated at such a glorious vantage point, was a Home for the Blind.

I sat there one day and pondered about it. Was it a waste of valuable land on a valuable site? After all, could it not have been built on some derelict waste land somewhere? Did it matter about the view, the outlook? Who would know, and anyway who would care?

Well I'm glad someone knew enough and cared enough to build it where they did. You see, you could hear the roar of the waves or the lapping water on the sea shore. You could smell the tang of the sea and of the cornfield and flowers. Birds sang and walks were unhindered by lots of buildings, and there was for a part of the year the laughter of little children. Somebody had caught on to the Spirit of Jesus about going second miles and giving and doing; so much more than bare, mathematical and cold necessities.

Another thing I noticed was that whenever we passed the home or thereabouts, or had coffee in the little village near-by, we kept meeting and seeing the folk who lived there. I'll tell you why. Lots of people used to take them out, and you would see them happily stepping out arm in arm, obviously enjoying their walks. Yes, there were wonderful souls among them who seemed quite able to cope by themselves but I suspect many were only able to get out because of those kind folk who took them for walks.

I'm sure there must be someone near to where you live for whom you could go that extra mile; add some colour or scent to their lives, make it possible for them to get out, or if they really are housefast perhaps from time to time you could go in to them.

I know it would make a difference to them, and what's more it would to you too.

Prayer for the day
Lord Jesus, much of your ministry was one of healing and helping. Help us to continue it today and always.

AMEN

'THEY SAY'

I'VE BEEN TAKING NOTE LATELY of what other folk think about me and about you. If we really take to heart what they're saying, you know we really are in a mess. Perhaps the best thing I could do, if what they say is true, is to throw my hat over Tower Bridge — and forget to leave it loose.

'They say.' Let them say! 'They say' is a liar. But they do say, and they suggest that we're one degree under, and we've got an energy gap; we ought to have a ring of confidence and join a certain set of men. They say we're all off peak or have weight problems, and if we're suffering from — Sh! you know what — our best friends won't tell us! Further, there are shades of whiteness, and cats who are nearly always kittens, and discerning dogs. And that sweet with a hole in it is best, when I personally would like more sweet where the hole is and more to eat and enjoy; I'm not too keen on buying holes when I'm shopping for sweets.

Well, it all gets bewildering because on and on it goes about where to live, where to go for holidays, what to wear and what to drive. The impression we're left with if we're not careful and don't pay due heed to all these assessments, the impression given is that we lack something. We're less than the best and most other folk are superior to us and we'll be left behind as worthless nobodies.

Well, fair enough. I know there are a great number of people superior to me and I know too some folk have got an inferiority complex simply because they are inferior. But when all that is said, where can we turn to find a true estimate of what we are and what we're worth?

I've no doubt where the truth lies: it lies with Jesus. He says I'm a child of God, and God loved me enough to give His life on my behalf because my worth and value belongs

6

not only to here, but also to hereafter. And what's more, He says the same thing to every one of you. Isn't that amazing? It's beyond logic and explanation, it can't be proved mathematically, and yet it's gloriously true.

A Cornishman who had hardly a penny to his name, yet he was a great Christian, used to dance up and down the streets shouting, 'I'm Billy Bray, the son of a King!' Yes, we are royalty if you like, and no matter what *they* say or try to say — we can look at Jesus for a true estimate of our true worth.

'He loved me and gave Himself for me.' And we can say it, for the very simple reason that it is true.

Prayer for the day
Thank you for your love, Lord Jesus, and for the knowledge that we are included in it and that it means that both here and hereafter, we are of eternal worth to you.

AMEN

RAG AND BONE

WHEN YOU'RE A MINISTER in the east end of London one thing you can be sure about is that life never becomes dull and monotonous. There's no danger of one getting into a rut and that rut becoming a grave. No two days are alike and you have the feeling that almost anything can happen any minute, and quite often it does.

I've found myself doing things and being in circumstances the like of which I've never encountered in a quarter of a century in the ministry before coming to Whitechapel.

Why only last week I added a rapier, a flick-knife and a studded belt to my collection of confiscated offensive weapons. I ran a tape measure round a fellow's waist, found he was 36 inches, and when he breathed if I'd struck a match we should both have gone up in flames. But the incident I want to tell you about was of a visit I made, this was the third or fourth time I'd been there, to a rag and bone merchant.

From time to time I go to see him with some things, mostly old rags and woollens that even we can't give away, and he gives me a few pence for them. This in turn is used for our work in the Mission. He's a fascinating fellow, well there are two or three of them, and they feel and finger the rags, weigh them, and then pay up. Often I have to wait my turn and I have time to glance around the yard. It must be one of the biggest collections in London of old tatty rubbish, rotten and rusting, and lying in every corner of the vast yard and buildings. All of it has been thrown out and cast away and believed by somebody to be utterly useless. In many cases the previous owners have been more than glad to get rid of it, to see the last of it.

Fair enough, so it should be, that's what scrap yards are for and they serve a useful purpose. But you know the scrap merchant doesn't regard it all as useless rubbish. For him it's all got a value, a true worth, and he does eventually turn all of it into money, into gold as the saying goes.

I like to go from time to time to that rag and bone man because most of the people I serve in my Mission would be regarded as rubbish, revolting, rotting and stinking, nearly every one of them. What's more, most other people think they have lost all value and that their right and proper place is on the scrap heap.

Isn't it grand to have a Gospel, good news, for folk like that and to tell them that Jesus doesn't see them or regard them like that. He never writes anybody off, never regards them as valueless and as having no worth.

For Him they are His, His own, a part of His family. As one hymn-writer puts it, 'the sheep for whom the shepherd died'.

I don't know who you and I are going to meet today, but no matter who they are, or what they're like, if we do mentally consign them to the scrap heap, make sure it is the one that Jesus owns. They'll be all right there, He'll see the gold in the dross.

Prayer for the day
Forgive us, O Lord, that we often make facile and wrong judgments of the work of others. Help us to remember that all men are of eternal and equal value in your sight.

AMEN

LOOSE COVERS

WE'VE GOT THEM AT LAST! Yes, in our house, over months if not years the pressure has been on me for us to have them. Plenty of other folk had got them it seemed, and I had to admit whenever I saw them, and they made sure to point them out to me, they certainly looked all right. What was drab and dreary became gay and colourful so that you see, in the end, I gave in. Well, men always do and the ladies love their own way, so after a bit of a meek show of defiance, a sort of gesture to preserve my dignity, we went and ordered them and they came by post. So I announce the fact this morning that we've got them at last: loose stretch chair covers.

Now I've got to admit that they strike you as you enter the room. My chair looks far more attractive now and they almost seem to have done something to the whole room. I've not the slightest doubt it's been money well spent and after all everybody's happy and that's that.

But there's nothing to stop me sitting quietly in my old chair and saying, to myself mind you, 'John lad, it's the same old chair underneath. I can still feel the spring if I sit too far forward and I know that underneath the cushion is burned where my pipe fell one day and I dropped ashes.' Covers on top, lovely, but, as I said, same old chair.

Come to think of it the same thing applies to our lives. A touch up here and there, Sunday clothes, attendance at church, holding office, writing Reverend before our name, or some other letters after it, wearing robes of office: a mantle of force or prestige or wealth or status. Maybe there's a place for all of them but we do well to remember that it's the same old me and the same old you underneath. The casual acquaintance may be taken in, as the casual caller may be, by our loose chair covers, but we ourselves know the true state of affairs.

Jesus was often telling his hearers of this danger, the danger of a cloak, a top surface, a veneer, and pointing out that it was quite worthless and indeed very harmful to folk who tried to denounce not only others, but also themselves. Christianity is not a matter of half measures, of polishing up on superficial renovation. It has to do with axes at roots, with inside as well as outside being clean, of full surrender, of new creations or being reborn or converted. It's not enough to say, 'Lord, Lord'; He has to rule as Lord and Saviour in our hearts. Then, and only then, are we worthy to bear His Name — the name of Christian.

Prayer for the day

Rid us of all sham and subterfuge, Lord Jesus, enter fully into our hearts and lives, so that we are all wholly yours. For your Name's sake.

AMEN

JUST YOU

'GOOD MORNING EACH.'

Yes, they used to say that in a Midlands town where I used to live. Sounded a bit odd to me at first and yet, thinking it over, it is a bit more personal, a sort of word for each individual, than 'Good morning *all*.' That lumps us all together, a vast number, a group or a crowd who is being addressed.

It is very hard in these days to keep this sense of individual and personal worth. The stress always seems to be on the mob, the crowd, and bigger numbers seem to matter more than smaller ones. Everybody is cast in lots today; the teenagers, the underprivileged, the Joneses, the third world, the Irish, the inmates, the unemployed,

When I worked on the railway I recall a dog escaping out of the guard's van of a train standing in Crewe station. A chain hung loosely from its collar and on the collar was tied a label. The guard ran down the platform after the escaping dog, shouting, 'Stop that dog — it's a parcel!' For him it was just one of scores of parcels entrusted to him and it had no other identity. It wasn't somebody's Fido, or Rover, or Bess at all.

At the Town Hall you're a ratepayer. At the police station you may be a prisoner. At the bus stop, the public, and at the football match, you are just the crowd.

Well, I suppose a lot of this is really inevitable but I want to remind you that it is never like that with God.

I'm sure you've seen, as I have, a man with his arm tattooed with a heart, and across it a name — Rose, Mary, Ruth. Well, a writer in the Bible says that God knows you and me just as though our names were written on the palm of His hand. Jesus too wanted us to know that we are all known by name and loved individually by Him. It could and should make all the difference to you today, and indeed always, if you will remember that for Him you are a person, known by name, and that you matter. In fact, believe me, you matter so much that if there had only been you, or me, in the world He would still have sent His Son in order that we should not perish.

Prayer for the day

We thank you, O God, that even though you have made all men everywhere, you still know us and love us and call us by our own name.

Especially help us to remember that for you we are never lost in a crowd but always in your sight and love.

AMEN

THE PROBLEM OF GOOD

ONE OF MY JOBS these days is as chaplain to the great London Hospital, both to the patients and staff. I recently met a new intake of young student nurses, sixty or seventy teenage lasses from all over the country. A day or so later a number of them spent an evening in our home so that we could get to know each other better. After they had gone that evening I began to think again about something I've often wondered on before.

'Why?' I asked myself. 'Why should these lovely young girls leave home and family and friends and come to live in what is not the most salubrious part of London, work hard and awkward hours, doing sometimes menial and distasteful jobs and not getting overpaid by any means and all for people they don't know, utter and complete strangers to them who are also sometimes quite ungrateful for all that is done for them? Why? Why?

In the open air, in brains' trusts and discussion groups, I have so often been presented with what is called the Problem of Evil. Why is there so much evil, badness, wickedness and the like in the world? There is no easy answer to that, in fact I don't think there's any full answer this side of heaven.

But I do want to emphasise that there is also a Problem of Good, as it were. Why do so many folk do so many kindly and generous things? Why are there still good neighbours about? How is it there are still lots of people who think service and sacrifice are to be preferred to grasp and greed, and gain and get?

Oh! I could easily give you a long list of those I've met who only do something for reward. Even in the church there are those who can't help in some piece of voluntary service

— they're not well enough or have no time — and yet they are as busy as bees both daytime and evening at some extra, well-paid, job.

I want today to salute that grand company of men and women, and thank God many of them are still youngsters, who do a grand job every day without any thought of what they will get in return for it. Their only interest is in service, in helping, in caring. At some point such folk touch all our lives, and we would do well to rejoice far more than we do about the great amount of good in our world, rather than to dwell too long and too often on the evil round about us.

Prayer for the day

Bless all the folk who day by day are trying to bring help and health to others and are not seeking reward except that which comes to all those who serve with joy and gladness. Help us to fix our minds more often upon the good around us and to add to it. For Jesus Christ's sake.

AMEN

'UP THE BLUES'

MY INTEREST IN FOOTBALL goes back a long way now. I used to support the Blues and before I could see over the fence round the pitch I've stood and shouted 'Up the Blues', many a Saturday afternoon. My team was Winsford United in the Cheshire League in the days of Fred Corbett, Dingy Berry, Jackie Walsh, Joe Yersley; and do you know I ran away from home one Saturday to go and see them play Macclesfield in the Cup semi-final. My mother gave me a rattling good hiding (applied psychology, I think you'd call it today). I never ran away again. But an uncle of mine said if I was as keen as all that he'd take me with him to Crewe to see the final. And he did too.

Isn't it grand to have something you're keen about, a cause that inspires your enthusiasm, something you'll back up at cost and at risk and with no thought of sparing yourself. Well I think it's grand, so long as the something is good and pure and true. I think there are an ever increasing number of spheres today in which all you can hope to find is pale, palid, placid, tepid, lukewarm mediocrity.

A fellow served me recently in a great London store and when he gave me my miserable parcel I leaned over and got his string and tied it up properly and cut it with his scissors and tied a loop so that I could carry it home easily and safely on the bus. All he did was to stand there and let me, as though he'd done me a great favour in serving me at all.

I went into another very famous shop here to buy some furniture. It would have been a sight easier to have pinched it. Nobody came anywhere near me, not a soul was keen to make a sale and as far as I could see I was the only customer. Needless to say, I came out without spending a penny.

What I'm pleading for is a pride of purpose, a zeal to do what you have to do well, to put all you've got into it.

There's an old tombstone in the south of England on the grave of the village cobbler and it says on it, 'Here lies the body of so-and-so who cobbled shoes in this village to the Glory of God for forty-two years.'

My own father was proud of his L.N.W. and then L.M.S. uniform. He polished the buttons regularly and saw to it for over forty years that he not only did his job but did it well.

And last, but by no means least, what about some zeal for Jesus' sake? There's no place in the Kingdom of God for pastel-shaded, mealy-mouthed Christians who are neither hot nor cold. We need what an old Methodist lay preacher I knew used to call, 'out and outers'. Start by making your mind up that in all you do, and especially in what you do for Jesus, you will be keen and zealous and dedicated utterly.

Prayer for the day

Lord Jesus, not for Thee my fading powers, the ashes of my heart. In the *fullness* of my heart I would for Thee be strong.

AMEN

WHO CARES?

I WENT TO PREACH on a recent Sunday evening in a Presbyterian Church to which I'd never been before. So before I set off I got out my London street map and looked it up. I knew the district and the name of the street so it wasn't difficult because there it was marked with a cross.

'Yes,' I said, 'that's it, that's what the cross means.' So off I set and there sure enough, right where the cross was on my map, there was the church I was looking for; all was well.

This set me thinking about the Church. What it is, where it is, how you recognise it. I knew full well that neither a cross on a map, nor the building it represents, are really the Church. In the end it is something far beyond a map reference or bricks and mortar or even stone, even though they be both carved and centuries old. No, none of these things, nor all of them together, really make the true Church of Jesus Christ.

I can best give you a glimpse of what is the truth of this matter for me by telling you a true and recent story.

A week or two ago it was nearly midnight and for once I was getting ready for bed and intending to have an early night. I rarely manage to get up and go to bed on the same day. It was then that we had a ring on the outside door bell. One of the old chaps who come along to us for tea and supper and a bit of warmth and comfort had come across a little lad of about eleven wandering about Liverpool Street station without any money and not knowing where to go or what to do. The old chap had decided that the little fellow couldn't be left there all night so he brought him along and as he handed him over he said, 'They'll take care of you there, lad.' Well we did, we rang up his home town and through the police put his parents' mind at rest and they collected him next morning.

I don't want to imply that my church is any better than any other, but what I do want to say is that if you ask me what and where the real Church is then I say it's where the homeless can find a home, where those who have nobody can come in out of the cold and wet and dark and find warmth and light. In a word, it's people who care.

It's heard all too often now, 'Who cares?' 'I couldn't care less, let them, the others, anybody, the council, the state, let them do the caring. I'm looking after Number One.' In a truly Welfare State you have got to have folk who care.

We should all start by caring more for someone, by finding someone for whom nobody cares. An old chorus used to remind us there are 'lonely hearts to cherish, while the days are going by'.

The longer I live, the more I'm finding people who are not longing for money, or things, or holidays, not for something different or spectacular or newsmaking. All they yearn for is to feel that somebody, somewhere cares. I know that God does and He wants them to know this; and maybe the only way He can prove it to somebody is because you are going to be a part of His Body, to do it for Him by caring.

Prayer for the day
Show me where there are those who are lost and alone, and have nothing and nowhere and no one, and help me in your Name to offer some loving care.

AMEN

HORSE TROUGH

THE THAMES EMBANKMENT is a fascinating place, full of history and associated with tragedy. It's a must for the visitors to London and it's bedroom for others who never leave London at all.

I've been down there many times and yet on a recent visit I saw something I've never seen before. It was a horse trough, made of stone. Carved in the stone it said it had been given by a Mr Bolton in the last century. I stood and looked at it and tried to picture it in the time of Mr Bolton. Large dray horses would rest from pulling their loads to drink there. Smart horses, with carriages maybe, and also horses with riders of good or bad intent would be equally grateful for refreshment on the way. The years passed by and who knows how many scores of times man and beast were grateful for the thoughtfulness and generosity of Mr Bolton.

But you know, if Mr Bolton came back and had a walk down the Embankment today he'd be in for a nasty shock. His trough is no longer filled with water but with soil, and on the day when I saw it the soil had flowers planted in it and the trough looked really lovely and colourful. I presume that through spring, summer and autumn now it brings colour to the Embankment. Yet it is not doing anything like that for which it was intended in the first place.

I'm quite sure that all of us from time to time do something which we think might well be good and helpful, as Mr Bolton did when he gave the horse-trough, and then having done it it seems to turn out a waste and quite useless. I've known some parents who feel like that about their children: all they have given has been wasted and become redundant.

Well, it isn't always like that. From time to time what we have given is taken and used in ways and for means utterly different from anything we ourselves envisaged at the time. Mr Bolton never imagined and never thought of his water trough filled with flowers.

The good we try to do, the helping hand we proffered, the kindly word and deed, may seem sometimes to have been of no avail and got lost somewhere as though they had never been. Yet, if not now then later on, some of these things may be taken and used for good in ways we never dreamed of, to help folk we never knew. I would go so far as to say that no good is ever all wasted. God would have us go on giving good things and then leaving them with Him to use as He chooses. It is not for us always to see the end product: it is for us to be kind and generous like Mr Bolton.

Prayer for the day

Inspire us to be kind and generous in thought, word and deed and then in trust to leave the final outcome to Thee, O God.

AMEN

JOHN JACKSON HAS ALSO WRITTEN
HELLO AGAIN —
ANOTHER MONDAY MORNING
and
MONDAY'S PRAYER ON THE AIR

published by Lakeland paperbacks

A cassette is also available from Pilgrim Records